MW01659614

FREE

FREE

Poetry, Dialogue, and Commentary of a Free Spirit

Andrea "Kitten" Perry

Free: Poetry, Dialogue, and Commentary of a Free Spirit
Written by Andrea "Kitten" Perry
Cover design by OrangeIsMedia

Published by D.O.P.E. Poetz Press
www.andreakittenperry.com

Original photography captured by:
John Dierre Welch
Steven Ray Coatley
David Price
Ajamu Clark
Leon Orange
Foreword by Keith Rodgers
ISBN: 9780997170108

DEDICATION

For Pharoah Haneef, because all that I do is dedicated to you.

For Michael, because you have been encouraging me to publish my book for the past four years. I have arrived.

FREE

Table of Contents

FOREWORD

First off, let me say that I feel honored to be asked to
write this foreword!
Although it will be more than four words.
I promise you that you will be looking forward
To reading the next poem and so on
This collection has poems that will shake you,
Statements that will wake you
And words that will take you
On a ride that is unbuckled with no speed limits!
Sort of like life,
Sort of like love,
Sorted, hot love…
That kind that's cool
To reminisce about to your present lover
Letting them know that your past is a gift
That can be used and reboxed for future usage between
the two of you…
Between the sheets…
Between the heartaches and heartbeats!
"Reelism" that you've been fishing for!
It baits you and hooks you!
In the end, it feeds you.
Just like you read each piece,
In the end, each peace reads you!

-Keith Rodgers,
Founder and CEO of Black on Black Rhyme &
The Back Talk Poetry Troupe
Host of Tallahassee Nights Live

FREE

PREFACE

By ANDREA "KITTEN" PERRY

The first time I was told that I could publish a book of my poems was when I was in the third grade. My teacher told me that I could, so I believed her. I wish I had done it at that tender age of seven years old, but here I am 21 years later finally publishing my first book of poetry. All this time, I feel as if I have been yearning for something that has been inside of me all along.

I think that's what we all do though. We search and search for that something to fulfill us, but if we would just take a moment to look inward, we would find that we already possess all that is required to realize our greatest power.

Many that know me know that I've been writing practically all of my life. Many know about my love affair with poetry. Many don't know though about my journey to publishing my own book. I've written in countless personal journals since I was a child. My work has been published in newspapers, magazines, yearbooks, blogs, and other forms of print. I've even started and stopped the process of writing my book a number of times. It has not been until now that I've taken the action to follow through with putting an actual published book out there into the universe.

I chose "Free" as the title of this book, because that's how I feel...in every sense of the word. I am free to be me and do what I want to do. I am free to write how I want to write without any restraints, talk about the subjects that matter to me, and flow how I want to flow. I am free to be quirky, curious, spontaneous, happy, accomplished, thankful, vulnerable and unapologetically successful.

I've had much success in my life. I've been very positive and inspiring to others through sharing my achievement and helping others to hone in on their skills and goals. Somewhere along the line, I lost that. For a long time, I had been stifling my thoughts and talents and living my life defeated. I had been living and working towards someone else's dream and kept putting mine on the backburner. I had associated myself with people who didn't support my dreams and people who were jealous of my accomplishments. I lost my sense of "me." I am grateful that I was able to remember who I am and what I am capable of...thus, this book.

In this book, I share some of my thoughts, poems, jokes, and art. These pieces will make you think, nod your head in agreement, motivate you, make you smirk, make you laugh, and hopefully make you proud. I write from my experiences and what I've observed in the world.

It is my great hope that with this small act of sharing my writings (which is big for me), I can inspire someone else to scratch that itch they've had for so long. Regardless of what setbacks you've had, what opposition you've had to fight through, or any obstacles you've allowed to hold you back, you can start now and achieve your greatest dreams. I'm just a poet. I write poems and strive to right wrongs. One thing I know for sure is that it's my time and your time. Join me in being *Free*.

CHAPTER ONE

FREE FLOW

House

I saw you that summer afternoon at that
coffee shop on the west side of town
Sipping my white chocolate mocha on my
laptop, vibin' to the cool music the DJ was
playing, eclectic sound
House...
We wouldn't play that...
House...
Let's leave it up to the DJ...
As he'd replay

Songs of love and freedom and strength
and peace
In that moment, hurt and pain and lies
would cease
As I watched you glancing at me from my
peripheral, side eye
I simultaneously ignored you, not a chance
of revealing a wide eye
Yet still, I wouldn't hide, I
Looked up as you approached me; you
stumbled when you asked me for the code
to the Wi-Fi
And with my reply
Somehow, you thought I lied
I'm sorry; I'm not a nerdy, computer
genius like you. I didn't know that for

everyone, the password was the same
Oh what the hell! You still asked my ignorant ass, "What's your name?"
And from that moment on, we took to dating
Sometimes... I mean, once in a while... As long as I wasn't busy and responded to your texts... Maybe
It was mysterious
I admit I left you curious
Let's take this thing right here slow
But as the months flew by, I found myself letting my restraint go
House...
We wouldn't play that...
House...
In my head replaying all the sounds of liberation from when you took me to House in the Park...
Let's leave it up to House in the Park...
As those DJs shared tunes that were sure to spark
Love and unity and oneness
And hope and faith and abundance
Somehow, I'm loving you; how did I get here now?..
How could I allow you to break through my barriers and release my fear, how?
Did this happen? Arrow wound is evidence

left embedded on my heart
Now, the tide turns; you show reluctance to being open to love, what sweet tragedy, wicked art
And Janet tried to warn me; she said "That's the way love goes"
Once you bear your soul and get naked, the other's ready to put on clothes
Stuck in love
When I don't even recall how I got all up in love
In the first place
And when exactly did this happen? Was it a Wednesday or a Thursday?
Roles reverse
Unable to keep my cool, I could quench it, but I chose the thirst
And you, that was like three years ago, but you still refer to your divorce
I wish you had mentioned the trust issues before you let me fall for you
I wish you had shown signs of insecurity before I gave my all to you
I wish I had sensed that your belief in God was dependent on mine
My mother told me to never love a man more than he loved me, so I was out of time
House...

We wouldn't play that...
House...
I just left it up to the CD gifted to me by your best friend, the DJ...
And I gave you so much leeway
As we sat in IHOP right before pancakes, while we pray
Should have prayed more
I'm gone and there's no turning back; I want more
I refuse to wait for you to love me
Now, you love me
Now, I'm your everything, nothing above me
It's like magic
But I admit it's pretty tragic
'Cause all of a sudden you want to commit to me when I'm no longer an addict
Why couldn't you just admit
That I was the girl that made your heart smile
And I was the girl that could take you that mile
When I asked you if you loved me when I thought that I was losin' you
I disappeared to find out you loved me all along, but those three little words eluded you
I never ever meant to play House.

[Verses & Vodka in Mobile, Alabama]

I Would Die For You

1100 feet per second

Jumped right in front of the bullets of that nine millimeter Glock

They had your name on them

Shame on him

For firing at you off some petty shit

I was your ride or die trap queen on a Fetty tip
Without the trap

See, the only game we were in was rap

Poetic Rock Stars, the only gang we were in was that

The only shots fired were in a battle

Leaving our opposition dismantled

But for this snake, it was inevitable for him to rattle

Sure enough, he showed how shady he could be

And somehow I proved how much unlady I could be

Diving for your life

Striving for your life

While he could give two fucks out jiving for your life

See, he thought it was a game

While we...we were on top of the world, rising to the occasion

Week after week, competition after competition, mics we stayed blazin'

Making crowds roar as we ate at opponents' core; their comebacks never fazin'

Us

See, we had a certain trust

That we would get on that stage and deliver and bust

Like we would shit on that stage, and to win was a must

See, we were a team

I rooting for you and you for me

And I remember saying I would die for you

And I always told you that I would die for you

And my actions showed you that I would die for you

I remember when we used to sit on the stoop and write poetry together

At age nine, you were my intro to hip hop, thought that shit would last forever

Fast forward to fifteen, graduated to raps and who had the coldest delivery

You had the hottest hooks, so you pushed me to release my inner beast

We entered our first rap battle together; we performed back to back

You had mine; I had yours; Nobody was touching us when we attacked

So we kept spittin,' and years flew by

Still flowin,' still showin' that we would fly

Because of our history, I would die for you

I am my brother's keeper, and I would die for you

Life couldn't be much sweeter, and I would die for you

And then there it was: the night of the final street war

Supposed to be more-so with words than a heat-war

Maybe he should have gotten beat more

As a child

Maybe his mama let him run around too wild

Maybe he was a product of tough upbringing, raised by the streets

Maybe he was never schooled to be a real gangsta when it came to packin' heat

Maybe he didn't know the street code

Or maybe he was a punk that got picked on in school when he was young, dying to fit in as he got old

But still livin'

The gift of life taken while still givin'

Off jealousy

Never realized a man's pride would be the hell of me

And I don't blame you for killing him off with your bars

And I don't blame you for spittin' dope and hitting hard

I don't blame you for goin' at his throat

Like B Rabbit embarrassed Papa Doc third round in 8 Mile, we watched him choke

It's his fault he couldn't handle the heat; he should have stayed away from the fire

He should have never entered this battle; he should have hung his gloves up and retired

How could a man be so moved to take
another man's life over losing a fight with
lyrics

How could a man be so humiliated? Not a
good sport? Take it so personal that it
messes with his whole spirit?

That it could make him that angry to pull
the trigger with aim?

Black Lives Matter... I guess except when
we have beef with our own, and we envy
their fame

This aint Chiraq...This aint gang-related;
this can't be life

This aint life...at least not mine...

1100 feet per second

Jumped right in front of the bullets of that
nine millimeter Glock

They had your name on them

Shame on him

For firing at you off some petty shit

I was your ride or die trap queen on a Fetty
tip
Without the trap

See, the only game we were in was rap

Poetic Rock Stars, the only gang we were
in was that

I still don’t know how I reacted so fast; it was reflex

Why do they call it ride or die when as I'm riding, I'm dying

There’s not a choice

I never got that

I did both.

And I proved that I would die for you

I know you’re mad about how I would die for you

But I’m resting in peace knowing you have another shot at life now.

Infatuation With Me or With My Poem

Is his infatuation with me or with my poem?

Or does the fact that I spit poetry hit home?

Or is it love, actually? Could it be? He says it’s been going on for years

He said I've been in his mind's eye before
he even had the fear

Of losing me to another John Doe

That's deep, 'cause that means he had to
have envisioned me before he even knew
what I was on though

Before the poems and seeing me
vulnerable on stage

And because he was a poet, he could relate
to me; we were overstanding that stage

But for me to believe that he could be in
love versus mere infatuation is a stretch

How do I know he's not a dog looking for
me to throw him a little bone versus being
the perfect catch?

I don't, and I'm not trying to be a pessimist,
but I've been through this before; ask
Gregory

Praising me

Doesn't require much bravery

Because all he had to do was say to me,

"I've been waiting so patiently

For my turn,

And I've learned

If you sit back and let it burn

With time, you will have what you most discerned"

But love unearned

By going through some shit like historically Black fraternity linemen do

Won't truly win hearts; mine must be won by hunting as man was designed to do

A chase so cold, have me writing rhymes that's new

And by the time I'm through

Have 'em knowing exactly what the love grind could do

Is he infatuated with me or with my poem?

Or does the fact that I spit poetry really hit home?

He met me at the poetry spot

I couldn't tell if he was diggin' me 'cause my poetry's hot

Or I was hot

But discouraged, I was not

Or should I be flattered?

That's the price you have to pay when you have the ability to move crowds, but talent shouldn't matter

And your fans are your fans

And doesn't it make sense that if I have a man,

He'll be my number one fan?

So it's possible for him to love me and my poetry

I just can't fathom the thought of him professing to me that he was in love with me without even knowin' me

That's what gets me

He saw me; I understand that I was pretty

But can a man just look at a woman and really see his wife, hear her speak and see into her soul

And just know

That they will forever be mates

Before first dates?

I'm still trying to figure out if that "love at first sight" shit really exists

Ad I'm still fucked up by the fairy tales I was exposed to as a kid

But I guess if I don't love and hurt

This infatuation with my poetry or this
"true love thing" will never work.

Eclectic

You are House in the Park on Labor Day
Weekend; you are the graffiti-walled
streets of Little Five Points

You are reggae on the patio at Apache
Café, Rasta Man's rolling up five joints

You are an open book, you free-spirited
soul

Running free and out of control

You can be tamed, but you don't wanna be

You are the freedom to choose who you
wanna be

You are full of love and grounded in peace

You are family: daughter, father, cousin,
and niece

You are Andre 3000 and Janelle Monae:
funky, cool, classic

Upbeat and relaxing

You are jazzy, rhythmic sounds of Africa with an island vibe

Salsa at Nuyorican in Puerto Rico, swingin' to that jive

Dancing in the rain, no inhibitions, free to fly high

You are floating on the clouds beautifully, colorful like rainbow's tie-dye

You are different in a world where so many are the same

Some may say weird, but you leave your mark and they forever remember your name

You are Lisa Bonet in *A Different World*

You are love and light to boys and girls

You are Pharrell Williams and Jimi Hendrix

You are the Sound Table where DJs spin, mix

You are DJ Maximus, DJ Kemit, and DJ Funsoxx

You are kinky, curly, wavy, nappy, afros, ponytails, buns, locks

You are artistry, creativity, ground-
breaking news

You are *Creative Loafing*, Mood's Music,
and Chuck Taylor shoes

You are Urban Grind, underground, the
nooks in Amsterdam, Netherlands

You are forever young like Peter Pan in
Neverland

You are full of life and energy

You are a mixture of a wide array of dope
influences, perfect synergy

You are old school meets new

What a divine infusion are you

You are ancient, but original

You are Ethiopia, indigenous, aboriginal

You are composition notebooks in back
pockets

You are the definition of expression; you
rock it

Electric like sockets

You are diverse with individuality

You are humbled, the truth, no fallacy

You are in the moment; you live carpe diem

You breed success; knowledge you feed 'em

You speak for those who didn't know they had a voice

You represent just being you and making that conscious choice

You are exactly who you are supposed to be

You are Eclectic!

Pay Yo Dues

If you wanna get with me, you gotta pay yo dues

If you wanna get with me, you gotta pay yo dues

If you wanna get with me, you gotta pay yo dues

If you wanna get with me, you gotta pay yo dues

No, no... it aint that easy

Just because I like massages and you think your chocolate kisses please me

And you hope that if you tease me

I'll fall victim to your trap and act sleazy

But believe me

I catch 'em early trying to deceive me

I aint naïve, see

I know when brotha just wants to have sex and leave me

'Cause I've been through it from one-night-stands to fly-by-nights

From trifling exes to bye-bye flights

From dirty brothas with STDs to fake brothas with useless degrees

From the sloppy to the bossy to the condescending one that cost me

My money and the price of a broken heart

No, a stabbed, torn, damaged, "I can't love no more I aint jokin'" heart

But not so much more of a "Yeah, he can get it if he be strokin' heart"

I got a copin' heart

And I'm learning to cope with my disparities

And I'm finding clarity in my life and from my friends that were there with me

At my time of strife, at my time of pain

At the point of time when nothing but revenge was on my brain

And they helped me to get through the storm

Holding both of my hands with God holding my arms

And they helped me to bypass the self-inflicted harm

And regain my courage and charm

So I'm saying

If you wanna get with me, you gotta pay yo dues

If you wanna get with me, you gotta pay yo dues

If you wanna get with me, you gotta pay yo dues

If you wanna get with me, you gotta pay yo dues

Because I am a better person now, and I understand how great my worth is

Not subsiding to this illusion of a kingdom telling me I'm worthless

Refusing to be bamboozled anymore, because I'm too smart for that

No longer using my body as an instrument of lust

I'm rehabilitatin' the cat

And I'm concentratin' on that

So if you're just trying to have sex, stay back

I said if you're just trying to have sex, stay way back

Because I want you to get to know me

I mean, I need you to get to know me

And I'm not saying cause I was hurt that I'm feeling like you owe me

I'm just saying console me

And don't be afraid to hold me

Get to know me

And don't be afraid to unfold me

Because once you know me,

That's when you really begin to understand

That I'm good all by myself, but I'm even better with a good man

And I don't need you in my life unless you got a good plan

Forget selling dope; I'm trying to get out the hood, man

Because if you wanna get with me, you gotta pay yo dues.

Antares

I love you, but I don't even know how to pronounce your Facebook name

Is it Ann-Taurus? On-terres?

You're beautiful, you goddess

Weird just when I thought I was the oddest

I found my match in you

And we be matchin' too

Wild child, natural hair, with the ratchet blue

You're incredible. You inspire me to be greater.

You're indelible, never could forget how you served me like a waiter,

But wait up

How is it that such a beauty as you came into connection with me?

I be knowing I'm the ish, but you confirm I'm blessed to be

Here with you, lovin' you

You East Indian princess, check what the government do

Now that we have the freedom to say "I do"

Let me give you this crown, my queen, and run this ring by you.

[Art Mondays in Atlanta, Georgia]

Content

Are we all sharing content
Or are we content
That our net worth is just gonna grow
With no correlation to our network?

A to Broadway

We hear it all the time:
"Ya'll should be on Broadway"
"I've never seen poetry like this before
But ya'll do it in such an odd way"
"You're phenomenal; I can tell you work hard, no off days"
"Why are you in such a small café? You need to connect to Barclays"
What they don't know is about all the hard days
We've had to endure to get to where we at now
Closer to the dream, but still a far ways
To go
And though we struggling, we prove and

show

That we're working and we 'bout ready to blow

So, let's do it, baby, let's go

But then life keeps happening

I'm pregnant, and his life keeps unraveling

City to city, getting stuck, unable to feed ourselves while we're traveling,

But we keep traveling

Rent is due; I'm fed up

I quit my job to pursue this dream, and now I can't keep the bread up

Replaying that song over and over when Tupac said, "Keep your head up

Even when the road is hard, never give up"

Even that's not enough now

Life's getting too tough now

Bills accumulating, starting to be too much now

It's hard to live off a dream

When the dream aint bringing' in green

And you're working overtime to build something, and the limelight aint what it seems

All those good feelings and all the standing ovations

Only further driving me to insanity when I come home from that temporary vacation

Because my family's looking at me like "get your life together," and they just don't understand

That I'm doing what I love, but who am I kidding? I need to come up with a better plan

That's it

No longer can I bear the pain of my sacrifice; I quit.

<u>Note to Reader: Times get tough, but NEVER ever give up!!!</u>

Naked

I want a husband

I want a husband who will love me

I want a husband who will love me naked

I want a husband who will love me naked in the morning

Break of dawn

Yawning

Naked at night

When it's dark out, absence of light

Naked

All of me

A husband to love all of me

"Beautiful Goddess," he'd be callin' me

With no makeup on

Tired of the nights I'd go to sleep with it caked up on

My face

Only to wake up the next morning with no trace

Of my identity

I want a husband who finds comfort in my divinity

A husband that will love me 'til infinity

When I am old

I want husband whose gonna love me bold

With no limits, no boundaries, naked

No gimmicks, no playing around with [my head and my heart] these,

Naked

I want a husband that will love my hair natural and curly

Or straight and girly

Naked

I want a husband that aint gonna fake it

Naked

I want a husband that will see right through me

A husband that will make the love and care of me his duty

Who will see me as more than just a sex symbol

Who will hold my heart as his emblem

For the definition of love

I want a husband who is naked in his spirituality, answers to none other than him above

I want husband that kisses the blemishes on my back and even the one on my left breast

I want husband that will love me to health instead of loving me to death

Lovin' me to life whether I do or don't decide to buy a new chest

Lovin' me

Even when I'm having PMS or feeling ugly

I want a husband that is naked with his fearlessness, accepting of self, confident, and strong

A husband to love me love me, love me, love me, love me, love me looooooooonnnnnggggggg

I want a husband that will love me naked, when I get out of the shower, dry skin

And when I go months without going to the beauty parlor, split ends

A husband to embrace my long fingers and my long toes

And my old woman hands and my white girl nose

And the way I snort sometimes when I laugh

A husband to love me still with mustache

Right before I wax it

A husband to love my ass the size it is, because there's no way I'm ever going "Nicki Minaj" plastic

I want a husband that will dance with me every day of our lives, even though I do it like Cameron Diaz

A husband to accept the fact that I'm not a model, I'm not an angel, I'm not a bad bitch, and I can be as

Quirky as I wanna be, weird, and eclectic

I want husband

I want a husband who will love me naked

I wanna

I wanna love

I wanna love me,

Naked.

Cookies

Who told you to put a price on that cookie? Yeah, I know Grandma's cookies are only 99 cents and you get two of them, but who told you to put a price on yours?

Don't say the landlord or the repo man or Sallie Mae like bill collectors make whores

One collector, two collector, three collector, FOUR

"But I'm not on welfare"

By all means, get on welfare if it will save you from your demise

Proud to be an "independent woman," but I can see through those rock-hard eyes

You are not free, but in bondage

Because with men, you never bonded

Before you opened your legs and sold your chocolate fondant

So although you dodged the bullet of being a victim

To the system

You still can't hold your head up high, look at your daughters at the end of the night and kiss them

At least not right away, because you have to wash your mouth out at least three times first,

Because you have to spread your legs at least three times first

Before the first

Your argument: "What's worse?

Having sex for free or making sure I'm getting my money's worth?"

But I say "If you knew your worth,

You would do a little research on this phenomenon called 'work,'

And you would look in the mirror and find value in God's work"

This woman's worth

This woman's worth is not being nourished by a man, so it's not fully your fault, sista

This is a result of fathers treating their daughters out in public as if they were their pimps and these daughters were burdens shouting "Come on little girl" to four-year-old Ebonies instead of "Come on, my princess" and taking her by the hand

Reassuring and affirming her that she can stand

Tall, telling her that 'she is kind, she is beautiful, and she is important'

It's bad enough that half our fathers aren't present, but when they are present, these little ebony beauties need to be exulted

So when they grow up like you and I, they will subconsciously know that they are queens

And won't be reduced to selling cookies to strangers like Girl Scout for green

But although it's not all on you, remember that you are in control of your destiny

Operate with dignity; test to see

How far you can really go when you discover your power

When you gain your self-love and our

Daughters begin to ask us if beauty is booties shaking on YouTube

And we can smile at them and say, "True beauty lies within you, boo"

And they will know and believe that they have it in them to make it and to keep fighting when it gets tough

That as long as they have purpose, that it's okay to struggle while they're finding their way when times are rough

It starts at home

And they should know

Queens don't sell their bodies out of desperation, and queens don't have low self-esteem

And queens don't sell cookies unless they come in a box and are labeled with a flavor like Thin Mints or Chocolate Creams.

MCM

You are the reason I'm blessed

Never would have guessed

That this between us could exist

Love between us could be bliss

You are the reason I'm blessed

Never would have guessed

That this between us could exist

Love between us could be bliss

Eternally my MCM, you are my Man Crush Monday

You create epic and exciting out of mundane

I knew that I would meet you one day,
But never before like this
God gives me new life every time we kiss
And after only five years with you, it's still so easy to reminisce
You inspire me; you got me focused like never before
I want to be the very best woman for you; I want to give you the world
And just when I think I've reached a pinnacle, you push me to strive higher
To have bigger desires
To think on a grander scale
To try again after fail
You make me want to be the best version of me; you make me want to build an empire
You inspire
Dope poems and eclectic lyrics
Hope, homes, and beautifully-hectic spirits

You are the reason I'm blessed
Never would have guessed

That this between us could exist
Love between us could be bliss

You are the reason I'm blessed
Never would have guessed
That this between us could exist
Love between us could be bliss
I remember that night I thought I almost lost you
Crying while rushing you to hospital
Praying that God would help us overcome this obstacle
Watching the man do what doctors do
Then there you were full of life
Smiling at me, assuring you were alright
And from there on out, all I wanted to do was take care of you
Be there with you
Because this scare wit' you
Was unbearable
And every time you tell me you love me is immeasurable

I treasure you
My miracle

You are the reason I'm blessed
Never would have guessed
That this between us could exist
Love between us could be bliss
You are the reason I'm blessed
Never would have guessed
That this between us could exist
Love between us could be bliss

And I can't believe we're here when before there was so much opposition
I admit I had second thoughts about you; I admit you were a big decision
With my mom and my sister tearing at me, deepening the wound, bigger incision
Making my mind chaotic, obscuring my vision
You came when I wasn't ready for you
But the most high said it was time; he knew

That I had to let go and let love, that our love would have no boundaries

And his grace would eternally be surrounding me

God knew that we would love freely

And deeply

And be connected endlessly, our beings

And seeing

That I trusted him, I am now a believer that love is not fleeing

It is gentle, it is kind, it is patient, it is understanding, it is infinitive

You are the beginning of my WHY: the equal to you making my purpose definitive

So I'm full of gratitude that you were saved: how I know his eye is on the sparrow

Something possessed me you would be my King, so I named you Pharoah.

You are the reason I'm blessed

Never would have guessed

That this between us could exist

Love between us could be bliss

You are the reason I'm blessed
Never would have guessed
That this between us could exist
Love between us could be bliss

Dear Brown Girl

Dear Brown Girl,
Don't be afraid to shine
Your hair is so beautiful
And your skin is divine
Your heart is full of love
And so is your mind
To think you possess anything less than greatness
Means you must be blind.

My Funny Valentine

Dear Valentine,
I know you're probably expecting this to be a poem about love, since that's what you asked me to write,
But the truth is that I don't know if I can take this any further past Valentine's night
And although we were already intimate,
And I know that I should be expressing more sentiment
About the subject—
But the truth is that before you, I would go on spurts of months of celibacy
And I know you're probably wondering what's the relevancy
To you
But the reason being is that after I become intimate, I tend to change my mind
I'm disinterested like you done gave it up too fast, didn't give it enough time to become sublime
Like a boy who got his head stimulated before she got to elevate his mind
Yeah, I admit, sometimes I think like a dude
But the truth is that I don't ever mean to be rude

And the truth is that I don't know what I was expecting; I didn't expect for it to be this good
I wasn't expecting for it to be Penthouse Suite; maybe I was expecting for it to be a little motel-hood
And I rack my brain trying to figure out:
'How do I tell you this?
How do I tell you that tonight will be our last kiss?
How do I look you in the eye knowing that you're about to be blind-sided?'
Knowing that glasses or contacts wrapped in red or purple tissue paper won't water the blaze I'm igniting
Dear Valentine,
The truth is that I don't want to hit you with another over-used cliché, but "It's really not you; it's me"
I'm beginning to think that I want to go on another one of my so-called sex-free sprees
But this time, seal it tight and don't conform until that ring is embedded on my finger
Because only then will I know that it's the real deal for me; thoughts won't linger
And feelings will never be hurt again
Dear Valentine, I hope we can still be friends

Because the truth is that I knew I had a problem, but I thought it would be a little different this time
I thought I could maintain a relationship with a man real and kind
And I know you probably need no further explanation or me treating you like charity...in kind
But I just want you to know that this is not on purpose
So for Valentine's Day, let's still do as planned
Let's catch dinner, repeat our first night, hold hands,
Gaze up at the stars as you hold me
And always remember the old me
The one you thought was different and beautiful
But the truth is that I know that it will never be the same again after Valentine's night, and maybe all of this is not suitable
So in order to cherish our last moments together as if they were our first, I'm going to wait until the end of the night to give you this collaboration of poetic lines and thank you in advance for a wonderful night...
My funny Valentine.
My funny Valentine.

The Flip Flops of Clarity

Day in and day out, being walked on,
collecting dirt and dust from the outside,
especially other people's mess

Trying to find solitude at the beach, but
even the beach is too sandy

When I just want to get up and go, they
come in handy

But for longevity, I have to continuously
cleanse them of yesterday's grime, because
unlike closed-toe shoes, it's apparent,
they're transparent

It's finally becoming clear to me that I've
been trampled on for far too long

It's time to rid myself of all the drama and
take steps towards standing for a better
me.

[Apache Café in Atlanta, Georgia]

Dreamer

I found out you were a dreamer; I
remember I once had a dream too

Now, I know why you seemed so familiar,
'cause in that dream, I've seen you

So creative, so colorful, of blues, yellows, reds, and one green hue

I saw your whole persona, your originality and knew you were a verb-spittin' fiend too

In just one lapse of reality, you became acquainted with me

It was a tainted fit, but see

With your unique spectrum, we painted it free

And like a bird released from being caged behind bars

We flew away and allowed our lyrical bars to touch stars

Together, we changed the game; no longer did women come from Venus and men from Mars

We united as one body, king and queen, and with our harmonious rod

We went back to our original beings, and we became gods.

Free Condoms

Free condoms: Trojan Magnum

Free condoms: Trojan Magnum

What? No? Nobody wants free condoms?
Trojan? Magnum?

Oh yeah, that's right. Because nobody's
having sex, right?

And no woman is saying "Yes," right?

Nobody? Everybody is saying no?
Everybody?

Well, if that's the case, there's no need for
me

"Miss PSA," I'll just keep these [condoms]
for me

But that can't be the case

With young men coming out of clinics with
distraught looks on face

But don't judge him; at the least, he got
tested...it was just kind of late

And don't judge her; at the least she got
tested...after feeling it burn, she let him hit
first date

That's okay; you don't have to live
protected, but before making that
conscious decision, first consider the HIV

rate

Every 9.5 minutes, someone contracts the disease

Ten minutes ago, it was spread, and someone just caught it again right now, so please

Consider using these [condoms]

And please consider using these...

Your brain

Because when it rains, it pour, and when it pours, it rains

If you're not protecting your temple now, it's time for a change

Set some standards, and I'm not saying that you have to abstain

But I am saying that if you leave reading this poem with just one standard, let it be to use protection every single time

Because all it takes is a single time

Get tested with your partner before consenting to having sex

And if he doesn't want to get tested, "NEXT!!!"

And if she doesn't want to get tested, perhaps, she has something to confess

Let's start a conversation

Let's talk about sex

Let's talk about all the good things

Let's talk about all the bad things

The AIDS, HIV, and the sad things

That 15-year-old girl who just contracted the disease after having

Sex for the first time with another infected teen

Who had just celebrated his sweet 16

Which wasn't so sweet

And now, every day of their lives is a gift

Because of a decision they made that caused a rift

In their relationship,

In their lives,

Because tomorrow is not promised

There are over 1.2 million people in the U.S. infected with HIV...

These numbers can change starting with you and with me.

Home is Where the Heart Is

Everything I write for you
Is to a "House" beat
Because my heart [beat] tells me
That I'm home with you

Space and Energy: A Tribute to the Mahogany Urban Poetry Series

This space and energy was filled with love and culture and creativity

And the positive vibrations we all felt through the airwaves were seen vividly

By souls that were intuitive and beings that were open to positive light

Our hearts felt the color of deep mahogany bouncing on inviting wavelengths throughout the night

We were all connected, kindred spirits, anticipating on sharing our ears and lending our emotion

Our insides dancing to the kaleidoscope of
music the DJ played, we were on a
rollercoaster ride unafraid to scream the
way we were engrossed in

The different genres that he would mesh in
with such vulnerable poetry, such indelible
poetry

Innocent, premature, aggressive, sensual,
revolutionary and incredible poetry

The room was filled with gratitude that
must have come from our ancestors as we
paid homage with Cleo's direction

I am convinced this sista knows something
about the universe; it's no wonder we were
so blessed from the show's inception

She created this force field of good vibes as
if Mother Earth herself was her teacher

This beautiful soul, she gifted me black
soaps and prayer herbs and tea that could
have passed for reefer

And she believed that I had it in me to take
dominion over my home and make it a
house with queen-like energy only our
foremothers knew about and tried to pass

down throughout generations, but somewhere along the line, it got lost

That night, Cleo Cartel brought it back. I mean, that energy lives within this Black woman, I felt her being stretching out to battered women whose lives have been for decades in holocaust

Broken men who were learning to finally be at peace with themselves after years of giving a piece of themselves

To a people who never gave a damn, stripping themselves of their man-given identities while opening up their souls to reclaim the crowns they had left on shelves

And the spoken words

Nouns on fire, flamin' adjectives, and smokin' verbs

I fell in love with a poet named Chris, because he spoke of oppression and pride, or perhaps I was infatuated with his poems; I don't know, but the fact is

He had my attention; and I'm not sure if he was African, but he had the best interpretation of what BLACK is

And the poet, anything other than a natural disaster, named Hurricane... He made my mom and I want to get up and transform into his backup dancers when he was talkin' that talk, jukin' and jivin', smooth and slick

And Blu, he reminded me of Love Jones, he had a way with his words like Darrius, he set the mood, the type a slow Maxwell groove would fit

I penned short, silly poems for poets and became intimate with these people that I had never met a day in my life; it didn't matter if it had been twenty people in the building

This intimate space contained energy that was illuminating as if it had been 1,000; we were one, open to connectivity, love yielding

I began to remember that I had known them for an eternity, because the way this universe is set up, knowing myself means I know like minds; we met long ago...this was only a reunion

The vibe, the culture was everything; "Ase" became my new affirmation; we exchanged thoughts and ideas and familiarities, both teachers and both students

The Dallas comedian and his accents, had me really trying to figure out what an "Elephant Nest" [LA Fitness] was, couldn't wait for the punch line

I didn't want him to get off stage; if it were up to me, I'd be laughing until the next morning's brunch time

And Khiry reminded me that poetry beef does exist outside of Atlanta, and there are poets everywhere who will attempt to infiltrate a culture and try to pass as the author of another poet's poem

Performing it with all conviction without giving credit to where it is due, as if there are no other poets in the room to call them out on their trife and let it be known

Derrick from LA was my muse; I took him as hostage, though I don't think he went unwillingly

The faces in the crowd all sang approval as we spit and we shared and we cultivated an energy that was equally nourishing them as it was fulfilling me

And that gorgeous light-skinned sista adorned with head wrap poured her heart out on the mic while Will gave us the 411 on everything arts and culture in the capitol

We listened and listened and listened and listened until it felt like we were taking a trip down the rabbit hole

Curiouser and curiouser, but I will never forget those three things that were spoken

And I will never forget the warm feeling in this vibrant ambiance and the pieces of Ethiopia that are the history of a people that can never be broken

We told one another we can do this. We will share our art, and creative energy, and feelings, and emotions, and passions. We will become poetry rock stars. For, we are already gods.

Marley

Little Nubian goddess, arms stretched wide

For me to pick up all 24 pounds of you

Light brown eyes peering up at me, waiting

For a gesture, a smile, a lift

As I adore your soft caramel skin

And notice your natural curl pattern through

Your platted locks and pink and white beads

You wear black and white polka-dotted leggings,

Tiny pink socks, and a white screen-printed tee

With hot pink and magenta ice-cream cones on it,

Tongue still blue from the raspberry-flavored Jolly Rancher you ate over an hour ago.

Hasan

Man Crush Monday since 2010

Don't even know if they had a MCM back

then

All I know is that he was sexy, and he
reminded me of Rakim

Not by the looks

Not the cover, but the content of the book

And that content had me so mesmerized,

'Cause he was a conscious King who
pushed exercise

He was a sexual being with lust in his eyes

But he was far more in-depth than most
guys

Meaning he wasn't shallow

And he was his own man, walked in
nobody's shadow

And he was far more caring, and he stood
for something

Justice, equality, human rights; it wasn't
just one thing

And he meant it when he said, "FUCK THE
POLICE,"

But he wasn't too naïve to think every pig
was a beast

See, he was well-rounded

Well-traveled, but still grounded

I could fall in "LIKE" just by the mere

notion that *Music Is My Weapon* was founded

But check this: he had the ability to make you wanna bone

And get toned

All at the same time, like "Should I burn this fat or take him home?"

Like "Should I follow his meal plan or sex him on the phone?"

Such a beautiful mix

I'm not talking about his *Life in Black and White* skin, those biracial pics

I mean what's within

Knowing himself, true to himself, loving himself

Shamelessly creating his own definition of wealth

A sexpert, personal trainer, MC, role model, and activist

Forcing the world to accept all of him

Not believing in the fall of him

Because he keeps ascending

And he keeps winning

And he don't stop

Like real Hip Hop

I love everything he stands for

He is Sensual Noire.

[Langston University in Langston, Oklahoma]

Maybe

I wish you were here I can't fathom how it feels

I have a longing for you, but I wonder if it's real

It's difficult for me to wait on

Something unknown, but maybe that means it's time to put my faith on

It's hard to maneuver

Through all the crap laid out like Hoover

I just need a lift, but it's too much to call Uber

I feel like I've been down this road

How do I know that this time will be breaking the mold?

If you can break down boundaries in your life,

Maybe you can tear down these walls; maybe you will have found me as wife

Maybe we can fight

In unison

Maybe I can give you a son

And adopt your daughter

Maybe I can be mother, you father

Maybe we can rule our kingdom

Maybe there will be so many other little things love springs from

But that's just maybe

A fantasy, a fairytale, a hope, a dream, baby

I don't wanna start nothing if it aint gonna be nothing

I don't wanna keep frontin'

I was dishonest when I told you I never thought about marriage; I was just trying to be hardcore

I don't wanna be exposed for the romantic I am

That's when men take advantage

If I can't protect this heart, no one else will place a bandage

Right there where it hurts deep down inside

Hidden feelings, too much pride

Truth is if you were here, I would let you impregnate me

I would let you hold me, let you date me

Let you in, allow myself to fall into your love

But you're up there above

And I don't know you

I don't know your mannerisms, how you move around, and it's hard for me to show you

Mine

And I get lonely down here.

Not The Way Love Should Be

He can't hear me. I can't get through to him.

This miscommunication has become usual

I dead him, funeral,

But now I'm tryna preserve him like, 'I don't want you to go'

And I just want you to know

That I think you're beautiful

And I think you're handsome

But I just wanna be assured that for my heart, you'd pay the ransom

Where you at? Where you be?

Working, I know faithfully

I just cannot wait to see

Everything great we'd be

Walking to you gracefully,

But I'm stuck wondering how you feel

Wondering if this is real

When I should be foot-loose and fancy-free

With no doubt that my man's for me.

If...You Were Wondering

If...you were wondering...I am not his trophy

This is not make-believe; this is real shit

This is not about playin' games with the organ that you feel wit'

This has been brewin' for seven years; I am finally ready for a good man

I almost gave up believing in brothas; I was on the verge of adding them all to a list of things in my life I would ban

This was not intentional; I walked right
into the sight of him and remembered

A feeling

That I thought was lost six months prior

I found it right where I left it, and he
welcomed me to acquire

It again...to keep...for good...this time...this
time...this time...he wanted it all

This time would be different, me, filled
with vulnerability, open to fall

He chose me years ago

He saw me in indigo

Like an African Warrior

I am not playin,' but I'm just Kitten

And he's just smitten

This is not some mid-life crisis

I am really perfect for him, to have and to
hold, his seed, his Egyptian goddess, like
Isis

More than every woman for him, serious
about building an empire on this solid
foundation we have laid

Together in bed; his dues were paid

No andropause, he is full of testosterone,

no pause, sex game on fleek

He warned me about this, and he made it to the top three of my top three, ex game don't meet

Or compare

To the lovin' that he's dishin' out

This is the type of fairytale shit I've always been wishin' 'bout

Since I was a little girl

It took me nine years to grow up after I was determined "legal" in this world

I guess you can now call this women's intuition...

CHAPTER TWO

HAIKU

Love Park

Recall when he took
Me to Love Park; I cried but
Love didn’t stay parked.

Bittersweet

He will not lie no
matter how much i beg him.
Truth is bittersweet.

Official

It's official when
he puts your son's name in poem.
Should have known sooner.

T-shirt

He left his scent there
on that tee he gifted me
He knew he'd go long.

The Man

Once boned a white man
He looked like Kevin Costner
Was no bodyguard.

[1015 Folsom in San Francisco, California]

CHAPTER THREE

LYRIC

You Liar, You Cheater (Fuck You)

You liar, you cheater. You lied, and you cheated.
You liar, you cheater. You lied, and you cheated.
Fuck you. Fuck you. Fuck you. Fuck you.
Fuck you. Fuck you. Fuck you. Fuck you.

I know I'm not a singer and that I could never be her

But when I saw you with her, it changed up my whole demeanor

I thought you were my man; you had me free and open like a dreamer,

But once I found out I was drowning while floating like Katrina

I couldn't believe my eyes; am I really seein' you while you're seein' her?

What didn't you see in me that you seen in her?

I wasn't lookin' for nothing, didn't even suspect you were a cheater

Could this be God's intervention? Revealing this villain, denying true love, like Jesus' by Peter

You liar, you cheater. You lied, and you cheated.
You liar, you cheater. You lied, and you cheated.
Fuck you. Fuck you. Fuck you. Fuck you.
Fuck you. Fuck you. Fuck you. Fuck you.

I understand she's younger, and I aint getting no younger

But I can't be naïve and believe your lies to feed my hunger

There is nothing you can say. I know what I saw, I will not be your fool any longer.

Can't willingly let you play me; that would just make me wronger

I realize I was weak wit you; thanks for making me stronger.

You liar, you cheater. You lied, and you cheated.
You liar, you cheater. You lied, and you cheated.
Fuck you. Fuck you. Fuck you. Fuck you.
Fuck you. Fuck you. Fuck you. Fuck you.

And even after all of our history,

You begging my sister to help you get wit' me

Telling her I was wifey and that this is it wit' me

Writing all that ill lit for me

When I thought I was becoming your decade, she was already your century

And they say the second time's a charm; you proved to me second chances aint worth shit

You became my whole world, but now I know how hard the earth hit.

You liar, you cheater. You lied, and you cheated.
You liar, you cheater. You lied, and you cheated.
Fuck you. Fuck you. Fuck you. Fuck you.
Fuck you. Fuck you. Fuck you. Fuck you.

Now, I thank you for this pain; I'm 'bout to blow up like Adele

Somebody tell 50 Cent that I'm ready to sign a deal

Just to give him hell

Make it all the way to heaven while this nigga stuck as that angel who fell

From grace, fell out of the race, so fall out of my face, and stop callin' my place

You will never get to hear my voice again; you are not worthy

I was out of your league for a reason, but I allowed you in to hurt me

So fuck you for hurting me

You muthafucking liar, you cheater, might as well had murked me,

Because I'm coming back from this dead relationship rising to the top, purposely.

You liar, you cheater. You lied, and you cheated.
You liar, you cheater. You lied, and you cheated.
Fuck you. Fuck you. Fuck you. Fuck you.
Fuck you. Fuck you. Fuck you. Fuck you.

Poetry Rock Star

We're not just talented for Broadway

But genius enough to rock crowds of tens of thousands like Barclays

Selling out arenas, then we re-up on our off days

Slangin' stanzas

While makin' 'em throw their hands up

And stand up in ovations

Tossin' liquor in jest, mazel tov-in, celebration

We deep, yeah, we so deep

Like Langston Hughes

Infused with blues

So to speak

Like Sonia Sanchez and Little Richard meets

Living out our dreams as Poetry Rock Stars

We're rallying with excitement, but this time burning down cops' cars

So we can win Oscars

For Oscars

And Grant Trayvons freedom from slavery

Like Angela Davis be

With her bravery

I'm a beast at this

Poetry shit

But my art aint for nobody to be cagin' me

I just wanna live free

It's my life; it's now or never like Bon Jovi
We on the run, Bonne & Clyde like Hov & Bey
Mixing rock and roll interludes with our poetry
I just wanna be known
For creating epic shit when I'm in my zone
Not put in a box
Following flocks
Confused about which way to hit home
I write what I feel, and I'm feelin' funky
So head nod with me, fellas, and ladies, shake your monkeys.

Cause I just wanna be a poetry rock star. I just wanna be a poetry rock star.
Oh I Oh I ...I Oh I Oh I.
Oh I Oh I ...I Oh I Oh I.
(Repeat)

[D.O.P.E. Show at the Art on 5 Gallery in ATL, Georgia]

Do You Think I'm Beautiful?

Do you think...
Do you think...
Do you think I'm beautiful?

Do you think...
Do you think...
Do YOU think I'm beautiful?

Tell me...

Tell me...
Tell me...
I'm beautiful.

Tell me...
Tell me...
Tell me...
I'm beautiful.

Do you think...
Do you think...
Do you think I'm beautiful?

Do you think...
Do you think...
Do YOU think I'm beautiful?

Tell me...
Tell me...
Tell me...
I'm beautiful.

Tell me...

Tell me...

Tell me...

I'm beautiful.

[Mardi Gras Café in Atlanta, Georgia]

CHAPTER FOUR

COMICAL DIALOGUE

(Mostly between me, myself, & I)

Old Boyfriend

My boyfriend is 50 years old. I'll mess around and marry him and automatically have grandkids. I didn't think about that when I first got into the relationship. Those kids aint calling me grandma though. Imma have to come up with a younger name like "Aunty Nana" or "Me-Me" or something. Hell...I'm still young.

My gifts aint even gonna be the same. You know how grandmothers pass down that one piece of sentimental jewelry? That one heirloom? Like for me, my grandmother passed down a diamond ring. What am I gonna pass down though? A blunt? "Hey granddaughter, let me pass this joint down to you..."

Sign That Your Baby is Ugly

I'm a waitress. When I'm at work, I be mad as hell when the hostess sits people at my tables with ugly-ass babies. I just be wantin' to say, 'GET THE FUCK OUT OF MY SECTION!' ...but I can't. You know what I'm sayin?!' So I'm forced to interact with the guests, like 'Heeeeeyyyyy ya'll...I'm Andrea. I'll be servin' ya'll today...Oh my gosh! He is so—look at his little sweater, it's so cute." Yeah, I practically have to make up a compliment out of thin air, because I can't say he's cute. I refuse lie...even if my tip is depending on it. I can't lie to save my life and say this little ugly baby is cute when I know he's one of the ugliest things I've ever seen. You know what I mean!?

I gotta figure out some kind of way to make a compliment to that baby, like, "Oh my gosh. Look at the way he holds his finger. It's sooooooo cute. Oh my goodness! Soooo adorable... how he holds his finger...ha ha." It's hard...All I wanna do is do my job, but these ugly babies make it so hard.

[*The Soul Lounge in Louisville, Kentucky*]

Ride

Men, get yourself a ride. It doesn't have to be a real nice ride...but just something that's reliable. My last relationship, I dated this man that didn't have a car, so it turned into me having to pick him up from his house, take him to and from work, then take myself to work, then turn around and get off work and have to wait for him to get off work to pick him up and then, I couldn't do anything until I waited for him to get off work. It just messed me up. I didn't really have a life after that. It got to the point to where I had to pick him up and drop him off so many places, I thought I was becoming his chauffeur, so I had to break up with him. So now, I'm dating a man that has two cars, and a motorcycle, a boat, a scooter, a bicycle, some skates...Man, I'm makin' sure that this man has some transportation. So if one thing happens to one of his cars, he's always got backup. I don't care if it's his skates, he's gonna have a ride somewhere.

I Know You Are Some-ting Else

I always get these random Island guys
an African guys too sometimes that
come up to me, and they're like,
"Where are you from?"
And I'm like, "California."
And they're so intense...they're like,
"No! well, what are you!?"
And I'm like, "What do you mean 'what
am I?' I'm a woman, of course...you
know."
And then they're like, "No! No! No! No!
No! I MEAN...WHAT IS YOUR
NATIONALITY?!"
And I'm like, "Oh, ummmmm...I'm...
American?"
And they're like, "I know you are some-
ting else! I know you! I know you are
some-ting else! I have seen you before!
You are not from California! You ask
your great-great-grandfada! I know you
are some-ting else! I know you! I know
you some-ting else! You look just like

my aunty! I know you are some-ting else!"
And I'm like,
"Ummmmm....uhhhhh...I'm...I don't know..."
And then I ask them...I'm like, "Well, where are you from?"
And they're usually like, "I am from the Virgin Islands..."
And then, I'm like, "Well, I'm from the Virgin Islands too then...if that's what you want me to be...since you know I'm some-ting else."
Like I never really know how to respond to these guys, but they always know that I am some-ting else with the hugest conviction in their hearts...
Like they be like, "Your hair! Your hair, I know you are some-ting else! You are not from California! I know you are some-ting else! You ask your modda! You ask your fada! Ask your great-great- grandfada! I know you are some-ting else! I done seen ya before, gal!"
And they're so intense, and that makes me want to be some-ting else...

Gifting Kids

You wanna know a way to get double your money's worth out of a gift to your child? Choose a gift that needs batteries. It has to be one that requires batteries to operate it. Wrap the gift up for the child, but the trick is not to buy any batteries for it. When the child opens the gift...say it's a remote control car...the child will be so overjoyed with a new toy and think that you're the best parent ever. Then the child won't be able to play with the toy, cause "Ah, man...you forgot batteries..." So, just let the gift sit for a couple of months, maybe a few months...whenever the time comes to purchase a new gift. Instead this time, you don't purchase a new gift. This time, you just purchase batteries. Then you go to the kid, and you say, "Look, Billy, I got you some batteries for your remote control car!" Then Little Billy thinks you're a hero and once again, you've become the best parent ever. I'm telling you this works. I do it to my son all the time.

CHAPTER FIVE

COMMENTARY

To the Single Woman

Dear Single Woman,

Let not your heart be troubled. Let your heart be still. Have patience. Your King is looking for you...No need for you to search for him. You know not how to look for love. You look in all the wrong places. Love should not be forced. It should flow—like the river. [He who finds a wife finds a good thing]—This message is not meant to be mistaken. It means you must allow him to be the hunter. In the meantime, much FOCUS should be on oneself and the betterment and enrichment of your spirit. Put much focus on your goals and advancement in all areas of your life. At the right moment, he will be shown to you...And you will be ready for him.

Poetry Was My Release

I could remember taking the streets of Atlanta by storm...and anywhere else I found myself traveling...Columbia...Charlotte...Oklahoma City...Columbus...Birmingham...Mobile...Ne w York City...Washington,

D.C....Philadelphia...and more cities...tour cities.

Yeah, I miss that feeling of being on stages sharing and caring and entertaining...Of making people feel good and comfortable and uncomfortable and good again...Of bringing out different emotions in audiences: the hurt, the pain, the sorrow, the anger, the happiness, the healing, the smiles, the laughter, the relief, the fun, the humor. Yeah, I miss that. Poetry was my release.

It's not just about poetry. It's about touching lives in the process, even if that includes your own.

[The Early Show at Erosol Dept. Store in Atlanta, Georgia]

Following My Dream

As a child, I'd always known I wanted to be a writer. Since I could read and write, I knew it was what I loved. I had read every book in our house so many times, I began to read the phone book and the dictionary or whatever else I could get my hands on. My mother encouraged and noticed my love for reading early on and would buy me children's books by Shel Silverstein. He became my favorite poet. I later graduated to read more advanced works by Maya Angelou, Robert Frost, and Langston Hughes. My love for a specific type of writing grew. My mother would buy me creative writing journals from Ross, many of which I still have in my possession as an adult. In these journals, I filled them with poetry and short stories.

As I grew older, I continued to write. I moved to Atlanta to attend college at Clark Atlanta University, and shortly after, I was immersed in the world of spoken word firsthand. After seeing the most beautifully-performed poetic collaboration by a poet named Las4Eva accompanied by a queen poet who was equally talented, I fell in love with it, and I knew that was what I wanted to do. I had performed poetry before at high school assemblies, but I was surprised by its popularity in this city. Coming from a town in California called Stockton, I had no idea there were so many different poetry communities in the world even. After showing my interest in spoken word, Las4Eva invited me out to perform at a bar called Apache Café where he hosted a weekly open mic every Sunday; it was one of the longest-running open mics in Atlanta. At the time, I was only 17 years old and too young to get in, but sometimes, it's who you know that opens the doors. I performed a poem there, and I felt a rush; from that moment on, I knew I was destined to not only be a writer, but a performer.

I began performing more frequently at open mics and eventually formed my own poetry collective (D.O.P.E. Poetz), started producing my own shows and plays, and also began touring from state to state, featuring my spoken word in different cafes and coffee houses. This became a way of life for me. It was like a dream come true. I quit my job and college (which I was taking a break from anyway). Though I was a struggling artist, I was having a blast.

Then one day, I found out I was pregnant. By this time I was 21, but still very young. On top of that news, less than a week later, I found out that I wasn't the only one. There was another woman that was pregnant by the same guy at the same time as me. I realized how fooled I had been and how unstable I was living...Reality... Check...

I had no job, no savings, no credit, and to make matters worse, I was getting evicted from my apartment.

The dream I thought I had been living no longer was an option for me. I didn't want to fight through it. I didn't want to keep pushing or believe that I could make it anymore. What had I been doing the past few years?! No degree...no real career... Who was I kidding to think I could live my childhood dream? I didn't want to have faith or believe that God would bring me through it and allow me to continue to live my dream...but sometimes you need a wake-up call when you're not living in your FULL purpose to your FULL potential.

I completely abandoned my life as it was. I moved across country to Oklahoma to finish college at Langston University. There, I got a part-time job as a waitress and cared for my son. I was no longer a performer. I got involved with campus writing institutions like Yearbook and The Gazette, our college newspaper, but something was still missing. On the day of my graduation, it was bittersweet. I was thankful I had accomplished and finished something, but I knew there was a large piece of me that had never really gotten a chance to officially begin.

It's a blessing to know what you wanted to be since you were a child and to grow into an adult and still have that same dream at your fingertips. Some people spend their whole lives trying to figure that out. ...And then I saw it. Someone had tagged me in a quote on Facebook. "The biggest adventure you can take is to live the life of your dreams." –Oprah Winfrey

I knew what that meant. I knew what I had to do. My son and I were on a plane heading back to Atlanta... back where it all began.

I started my own arts and entertainment company. This way, I could not only provide poetry-writing services and workshops, but I could also utilize my skills and love of performing in different industries.

Although I still have hard times and plenty of setbacks, I still know that this is the life I'm supposed to live. There are going to be tribulations tugging at us every step of the way, and I've had to make plenty of sacrifices, but the lesson learned in my journey is to never ever give up. Had I not given up, I would be further along in achieving goals relating to my dream than I am now, but I am certain that God has a plan for all of us, and life is as it should have been lived.

No matter what road you have to travel to get there, never give up on your dreams.

It's true that God won't put more on you than you can bare. I am a living witness of it. Keep going. Push harder. Fight more. Live your dream. Pursue it relentlessly. Giving up is not an option.

[The Early Show in Atlanta, Georgia]

Trey Songz Thinks I'm Bland

Trey Songz thinks I'm "bland." Yes, bland like boring.
So, I'm in college, and I'm about to walk into the auditorium when I see Trey Songz outside by the door. OMG!!! I keep walking. He stops me.
He stops me!!! We get to talking...and talking...and talking for a while.

We even take a selfie. Of course, I asked him to.

Then, he asks me "do you have more time...like 20 more minutes?"

DUH!!! Well, I did have something to do, but of course, I had 20 more minutes for Trey Songz. So, we go across the parking lot over to this bench on the grass, and we talk some more...about different things. I don't really remember talking about anything specific that pertained to me in particular. LOL...Don't quite remember. I was so overwhelmed.

So, anyway...he releases me. I go and pick my friend up from work. LMAO! Then, I think to myself...Trey Songz didn't ask me for my number...Damn. But there is something called Instagram...bam! Maybe I can post the picture of us together & tag him and get his attention. So, I do that.

I post the "ussie..." the selfie of us. I must have DM-ed him and asked him for his number or something, because next thing I know I'm doing is calling him.

Ring-Ring-Ring. He answers. I'm like, "Trey...Trey...do you think you can buy me a bottle of Rosé?" (LOL. Just kidding. I didn't say that, because I'm not Nicki Minaj, and I was not on the song "Bottoms

Up"). Ok so, I was really like, "Hey how are you?"
You know...the formalities. Ok so to get to the point...
Trey Songz asked me if he could be honest. I said yes. The very next thing that came out of his mouth nearly took my breathe away: "I think you're bland."
"Wait, what...like boring?"
"Yes...(pauses) boring."
(Heart sinking)
But he's such a sweet♥ and a gentleman...
He starts telling me what his plans were for the evening and about his show on Friday and said I was welcome to come to the festivities (but I'm sure he was thinking "keep your boring ass at home and away from me"). So, we get off the phone...on good terms of course.

I am actually glad that he was real with me, because I wasn't being real with myself...or with him. I was trying to act more reserved when I'm really a firecracker.
I was so worried about trying to be the furthest thing from a groupie that I forgot I'm not even a groupie in real life, so what do I have to worry about!? I wasn't being witty like usual. I wasn't being funny like

usual. I wasn't engaging and relatable. I could have told him that I entertained too & I was famous like him (in my own little ♥), and he probably would have laughed. I mean, isn't that something I would say to a normal dude?! And technically, isn't Trey Songz a normal dude?
I mean he's not an alien or anything. Honestly, I'm so glad that I know now that I can be my awesome self and not this "BLAND" perpetuator, because if Hill Harper is in my next dream, it's on and poppin'.

[Celebrities Nightclub in Vancouver, Canada]

Poetry

I love **poetry**. Poetry is from what I can remember the thing that saved me as a child...ever since I learned to read and write. I was never outspoken, except in my journal. I was excited to write. I was so quiet, but in my mind, I was a giant. I was this proud-to-be-black, intelligent little genius just waiting for the world to listen...And in my spare time, I read dictionaries and fiction and nonfiction and magazines...which later led to phone books and thesauruses and mail just because there was nothing left in my home to read that I hadn't already.

And my penmanship...I guess I got so much practice in writing that my handwriting was lovely at such a young age. My pencil was my microphone, and my paper was the stage.

I can remember my third grade [substitute] teacher telling me that I could be published...that my poems could be in a book too... just as Maya Angelou's were...just as Shel Silverstein's were...my heroes! My two favorite poets, my two favorite childhood writers...they influenced me.

You wanna know what influence is? Pick up a book and read. It's there in the great works of Langston Hughes. It's even there in Shakespeare.

And then there was Sonia Sanchez and Amiri Baraka...I still remember them coming to my school to speak...and recite poetry...and share their experiences with Brother Malcolm and civil rights...and The Black Arts Movement. Yeah, they were the truth. They were uplifting.

With Sonia, I never felt alone about expressing my sexuality and my thoughts on sex, because she...She was the realest when she wrote, and she was naked in works like *Shake Loose My Skin* and the likes. She was the truth. She let me know it was alright to pour out my heart of beds and passion on stage...yeah, she let me know it was fine to write of love and lust on page....and I began to think that age– was nothing but a number when it came to matters of the heart. Poetry was and still is my art.

CHAPTER SIX

EROTICA

[Mr. Tay's Comedy Twist in Stockton, California]

Fellatio

I think it's so true that you're still running through my bloodline; your cum was the best cum I've ever tasted

It wasn't sour; it wasn't tart...just right, and while giving you head, I felt time couldn't be wasted

So, I took advantage of the moment that I had with your dick

I touched and caressed it and wasn't afraid to lick

And suck and spit

And get it all wet until you said, "Quit"

And I bet you never would have thought I'd make you say "Stop"

You couldn't handle the good feeling; I sucked your dick like a bop-

pa...Like a boppa

And when you came, I swallowed

And even after, I still kept sucking your dick like there was no tomorrow

So I know your DNA is still in my veins

Because when I go to sleep, I dream about you and how I gave you brain

And how my mouth was so fixed upon your head, I almost gave you an asthma attack

Cardiac arrest or something, but I guarantee that after all of the health problems, you'll still be coming back

And I know you liked it how I came back and sucked you and swallowed two more times voluntarily

And when you asked me if I was finished, I was like, "Barely"

And I massaged your penis with my oral tissue

And I could have sworn I saw a tear slide down your cheek, so I gave you a tissue

Or that probably was just sweat, so you wiped that shit off

And I don't usually use my teeth, but I know you like it when I bite that shit soft

And I can get off just by sucking your dick

I mean, I get excited just off sucking your dick

I mean, I get aroused just from fucking your dick

And I'm sorry, but I don't mean to use your dick's name in vein

But didn't I tell you that your penis juice was in my veins?

And the next time I suck you, Imma lock you up in chains,

Because the way I had you running was like you got busted with cocaine

But when you busted, you came,

And I know you know that I'm a beast when it comes to that head game

Because I saw the way you were looking at me and watched my head go up and down,

And when you saw the imprint of your head against the inside of my cheek, no, you did not frown

You smiled

And I know you thought it was worth while

And you probably wouldn't give a damn if fellatio made a child

Because when a sista can suck a dick as good as me, it'd have a man going crazy like on *Girls Gone Wild*

I know you remember when I sucked a little, kissed a little, then licked real fast

Stroked some while rubbing your balls and making it last

And keeping it wet, because I know you like wet places

Like my pussy, but forget exchanging fuck faces

I was trying to give you suck faces

All I was trying to do was please you, and I think I did a Pro job

I knew by your expression, I gave the perfect blow job.

[Punany Poets' Classic Punany Cabaret Show, Philadelphia]

Do What It Do

I want to make it do what it do with you

Let's go to the tellie and make my coochie coo with you

I aint got a man, and I'm feenin' you

And you single too, so it's me and you

I wanna be in you

And you all against my walls

Feelin the wetness with every raindrop that falls

You be the leader, or I'll make all the calls

I'll drop my thong when you drop your drawls

Do everything to be pleasing me

And you aint gotta lick the clit; I'm down with teasing me

You're so sexy

Show me how your flex be

Show me that you're nasty

What you want, Papi, just ask me

Because I'm a freak in the sheets or on the counter or on the floor,

And we can do it anywhere, but I've got

too much class to be classified as a whore

I've just been thinking about what I want to do to you

Already freaked you on the dance floor; now, I want to put that chop and screw to you

Like that music in Texas

I know you want it, so come and test this

Give me a wet kiss

Come feel my wetness

I'll scream your name if you do it right

"Rodney...Rodney...Rodney" all through the night

And I hope you've got a lot of energy

Because you're gonna have to put a lot into me

And you're gonna know I aint the enemy

As soon as you enter me

So, come on, and try to center me

I'm having fantasies and daydreams about you

I'm thinking like you can beat it right and have me shout, "Ooooh"

I wanna strip for you

Be your private dancer and dip for you

Pull a tip for you

Make my ass-cheeks rip for you

I don't drink much, but I'll even take a sip for you

Kiss your sexy lips for you

Like a belly dancer, move my sexy hips for you

All I need is one night

One-night-standing...Oooh, I'm so tight

And I'll have you feeling so right

If you want me to, I'll bite

You can hit it from the front, and please hit it from the back

I'll ride you like the rodeo while massaging your sack

Have you all twisted with some Patron, Grey Goose, boy, give me some Yak

If you're always sexing white chicks, I'll have you sticking to Black

Have you forget about Port Arthur, Texas, go straight to ATL and never come back

Boy, you don't know about me, I'm always underestimated

Ask about me, so damn X-rated

And I don't even have to be throwed or faded

I've got a natural high

And my sex drive says I go 18-dummy, no lie

Sure hope you have extra condoms, because I have to stay protected

Sex you four times in one night, naked

Promise me it'll be good

Promise me your dick is so hood

Hope you like it fast, slow, and are familiar with the positions

If not, I'll be your teacher, so there won't be any collision

Sure hope you can drive, because once the key gets in the ignition

I'm telling you, if you're a pastor, you're going to lose your religion

If you're not blind, like Ray Charles, you're going to lose your vision

Because my shit is so bomb

It'll have you go home telling yo mom

"I think I'm in love with a poet; I wanna marry her,

Take my vows and carry her

Have a couple of sons, a phat house, and a terrier"

Boy, this is an offer that you can't turn down

Boy, I aint playing or trying to clown

We have chemistry; I'm serious

I just want to taste your body; I'm so curious

As long as I don't have it, I'm going to be delirious

So *Give Me That*, daddy; I'm trying to be like '05 Webbie

Put some whipped cream on my body, and picture me as Lil' Debbie

Whatever you're lookin' for, I got it

Sex 101: would you believe that I taught it?

You're so perfect, your body, not too skinny, not a fatty

Big and tall, just my type; I'll be your mommy and call you daddy

Forget about what society thinks; that aint got nothing to do with me and you

It's just the two of us when I'm seein' you

Aint no reason to be creepin' boo

Imma sex you all night and have you

sleepin' boo

Imma give you the business; I hope you can hang

Have you back at U of H telling your gang

About how I put it on you and how you want to bang

Have you wishing you were back with me, have you like "Fuck....dang"

Have you only wanting to fuck with Cali girls

Not the Southern ones, more so the Bay or the Valley girls

So, boy what are you waiting on? Come get on my hype

I just want to put some chocolate flavor in your life

I don't have to be your girl, not asking to be wife

I'm just feelin' you

And trying to keep it real wit' you

So celebrate with me; I'll drink to you and bring the confetti

I'm right here, Pa, so holla at me when you're ready.

ABOUT THE AUTHOR

Andrea "Kitten" Perry is an internationally touring performance poet and motivator, a 2016 Poet of the Year Nominee for the Northern California Entertainer's Music Awards, and published author of ***FREE: Poetry , Dialogue, and Commentary of a Free Spirit (2016)***. A 2012 Scripps- Howard Fellowship recipient, Andrea's work has been featured on V-103 (The People's Station) in Atlanta, KSBI in Vancouver, People TV, on tour with the Punany Poets (As seen on HBO), and more. In addition to performing, Andrea holds self-publishing workshops for those that are interested in writing and distributing a book and is one of the founders of D.O.P.E. Poetz, a troupe of artists formed in 2009 that live by the acronym: Delivering Outstanding Performances Every time. In 2015, Andrea co-wrote and published her first poetry chapbook entitled D.O.P.E. Dealers and has a Bachelor of Arts in Broadcast Journalism . Andrea resides in her hometown, Stockton, California, with her son, Pharoah.

Made in the USA
Coppell, TX
26 October 2021

64733071R00075